Online Safety

Phyllis Cornwall
and John Willis

DIGITAL CITIZENSHIP

LIGHTBOX
openlightbox.com

Go to **www.openlightbox.com** and enter this book's unique code.

ACCESS CODE

LBXW4894

Lightbox is an all-inclusive digital solution for the teaching and learning of curriculum topics in an original, groundbreaking way. Lightbox is based on National Curriculum Standards.

LIGHTBOX SUPPLEMENTARY RESOURCES

SHARE
Share titles within your Learning Management System (LMS) or Library Circulation System

CURRICULUM
Find national and state curriculum correlations

CITATION
Create bibliographical references following the Chicago Manual of Style

STANDARD FEATURES OF LIGHTBOX

AUDIO High-quality narration using text-to-speech system

ACTIVITIES Printable PDFs that can be emailed and graded

SLIDESHOWS Pictorial overviews of key concepts

VIDEOS Embedded high-definition video clips

WEBLINKS Curated links to external, child-safe resources

TRANSPARENCIES Step-by-step layering of maps, diagrams, charts, and timelines

INTERACTIVE MAPS Interactive maps and aerial satellite imagery

QUIZZES Ten multiple-choice questions that are automatically graded and emailed for teacher assessment

KEY WORDS Matching key concepts to their definitions

This title is part of our Lightbox digital subscription

Lightbox Grades 3–5 Subscription
ISBN 978-1-5105-5424-5

Access hundreds of Lightbox titles with our digital subscription. Sign up for a **FREE** subscription trial at **www.openlightbox.com/trial**

Online Safety

Contents

1 Chapter One

Online Safety Rules

Practicing safety means not doing things that could hurt you or others. It means staying away from danger. There are different kinds of dangers, even when you use a computer. In this book, we are going to explore **online** safety.

Be careful when you go online. Following basic steps can help keep your personal information safe.

Your school has safety rules that you are expected to follow. Not running in the halls is one of these rules. Not cheating and not damaging school property are others. These rules help students get along with each other. They also help prevent people from getting hurt in some way.

Nearly half of **students around the world use desktop computers** in the classroom.

More than **75 percent** of **U.S. classrooms** regularly **use desktop computers**.

School lunchroom rules ensure that everyone is able to eat safely.

Did you sign an Acceptable Use Policy? Have you ever seen it? A school's media specialist or a teacher can show it to you. Is it too hard to understand? Ask an adult to help you.

Read an Acceptable Use Policy carefully to make sure you can follow it properly.

Your school has computer rules, too. You probably signed a form called an **Acceptable Use Policy**. It lists rules you are expected to follow when you are using school computers. You cannot mess with other kids' computer files. You cannot download anything without permission. When you signed the form, you were promising to follow these rules. These rules will keep you safe on the computer.

Try This

Make an Acceptable Use Policy for your computer at home. Write a list of rules for you and your family to follow. You can look at your school's policy for ideas. Should you ask for permission before going online? Maybe you should limit your time on the computer. Type up your list on the computer. Print it out. Ask your family members to sign the paper. You sign it too! Post it near your family computer. Then everyone will see the safety rules.

Make sure everyone follows the rules.

History of School Computers

1970s
The personal computer is developed.

1984
About 30 percent of Grade K–12 students use computers both in school and at home.

Early 1990s
The **internet** becomes widely available to the general public.

2004
More than 2 million U.S. college students are taking at least one online course.

2009
About 93 percent of U.S. classroom computers are connected to the internet.

2010
Online class enrollment is 22 times higher than it was in 2000.

2020
The COVID-19 pandemic causes many U.S. schools to move to entirely online education.

Mapping School Computers

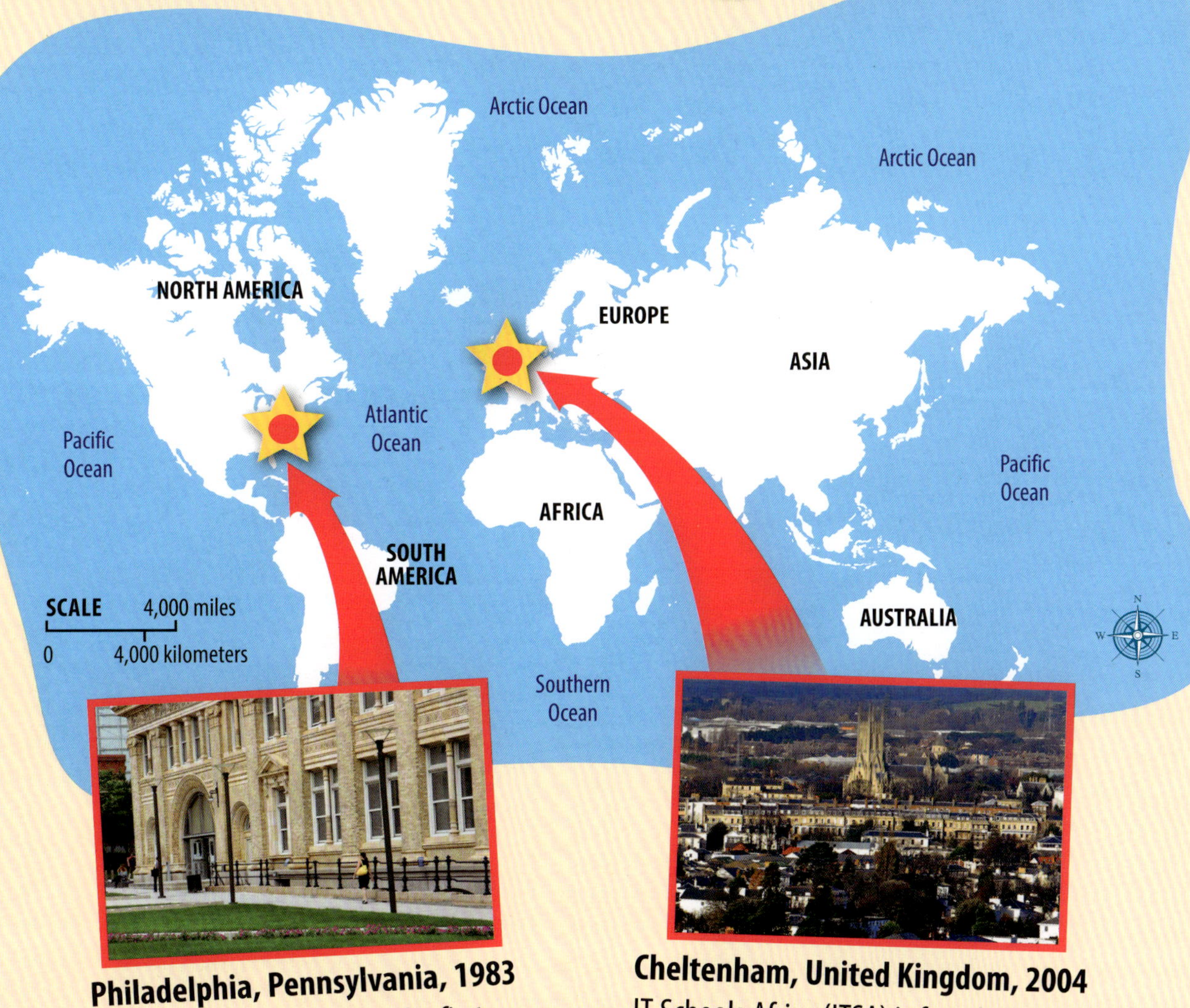

Philadelphia, Pennsylvania, 1983
Drexel University becomes the first U.S. school to require students to have personal computers.

Cheltenham, United Kingdom, 2004
IT Schools Africa (ITSA) is founded to help provide computers to schools in Africa.

2 Chapter Two

Online Privacy

Privacy means keeping some things to yourself. The words you write in a journal are your own thoughts and personal information. You probably do not want to share them with other people. The things other people tell you are their private thoughts and information. You should not share them with anyone else.

It is easy to keep other people from reading a journal. It can be stored safely where others cannot find it.

When you are online, you are connected to many other people. Strangers can read your words and see pictures that you post on the internet. Your friends or family might be embarrassed or get into trouble if you post pictures of them or things they said. Do not post their email address, home address, or the school they attend. Strangers may try to find them. Doing these things is not practicing online safety.

Do not be tricked. People do not always tell the truth online. Sometimes they pretend they are someone else. Sometimes they pretend to be nice. You cannot tell by reading their words. You should not trust them. They might be dishonest or dangerous. Keep your personal information private. That will protect you from pretenders.

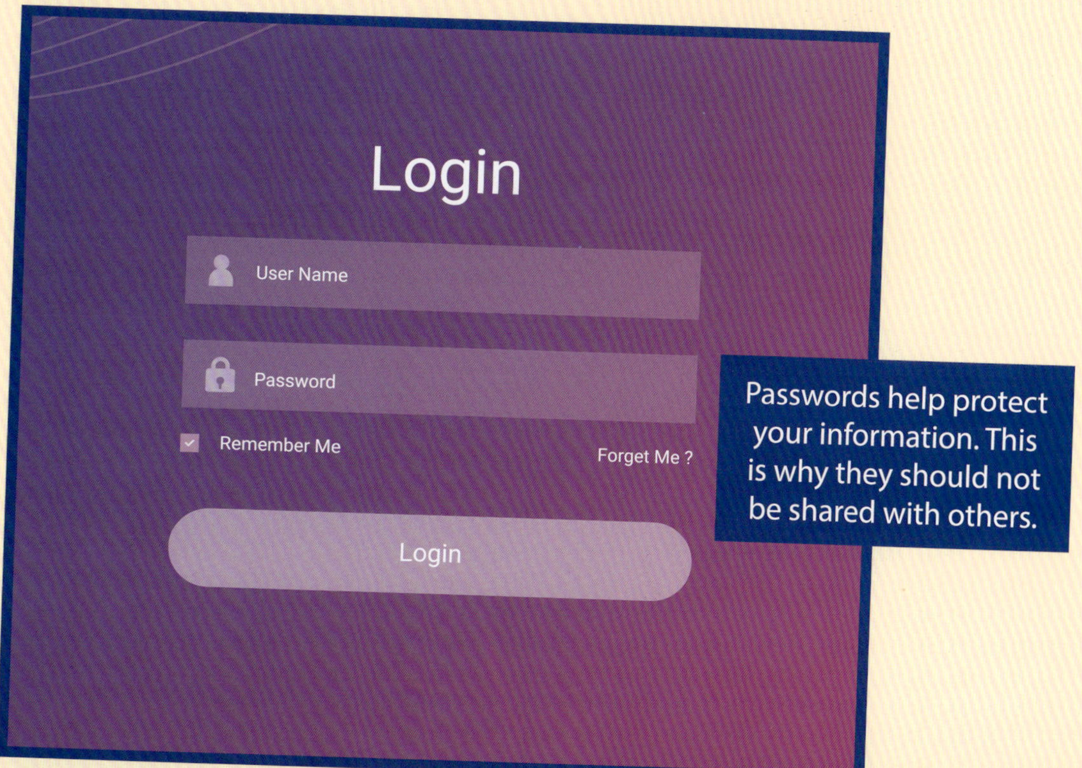

Passwords help protect your information. This is why they should not be shared with others.

Strangers are not the only ones who can harm you. Even people you know can cause trouble. They can see your words and pictures. Maybe you wrote about yourself. Maybe you wrote about your family, your friends, or your teachers. People might use your words to embarrass you. They might try to get you into trouble. Writing on the internet is public. Even places you think are private are not. Be very careful about what you write. It might come back to hurt you.

Do not post anything online that you would feel uncomfortable with any person reading.

Try This

Some information is safe to share. Other information is not. Can you tell which is which? Look at the list below. Are these things safe to share online?

1. Your favorite color
2. Where you go to school
3. What you had for dinner last night
4. Your birthday
5. Your name

ANSWERS: 1. safe, 2. not safe; a stranger could use this to find you, 3. safe, 4. not safe; a stranger could use this to figure out who you are, 5. not safe; never use your real name, especially when you do not know who will read or see what you post.

3 Chapter Three

Safe Places Online

The internet can be a fun and safe place to play and learn, However, how do kids find safe places on the internet? You will have to use your common sense and follow some simple tips.

Ask a parent or a teacher to help you if you are unsure if a website is safe or not.

Kid-friendly search engines are a great way to find safe sites.

Know where to look for safe websites. At school, your teacher can suggest some sites. So can your media specialist and the public library. Libraries often have **databases**. These are kid-friendly, safe, and **reliable**. There are also many **search engines** just for kids.

At home, always tell your parent or guardian when you will be using the internet. Make a list of each site you visit and show them the list. If you see anything online that upsets you, turn off the screen and tell your parent immediately. There is lots of information online. Not all of it is for kids.

Always ask an adult if you are unsure about anything you find online.

Try This

You can **bookmark** your favorite websites. This makes it easy for you to find them later.

1. Find a website that you like. Make sure it is kid-friendly. Ask an adult if you are not sure.
2. Go to the site. Push the Control or Command key and the D key on your keyboard at the same time.
3. Click "Add" or "Done" on the menu that pops up, or just hit Enter on your keyboard.
4. Now, find your bookmark. It might be at the top of your screen under "Bookmarks" or "Favorites." You might see it at the top of the window that shows the website. Click the name of the site you just bookmarked. What happens?

4 Chapter Four

Staying Safe Online

Dangerous places have warning signs. They let you know to be careful. "Wet Floor" signs keep you from slipping. "No Diving" signs keep you from diving into shallow water. Unsafe places on the internet do not have warning signs. You have to use your common sense. That will keep you safe.

Warning signs are clear and simple to help keep people safe.

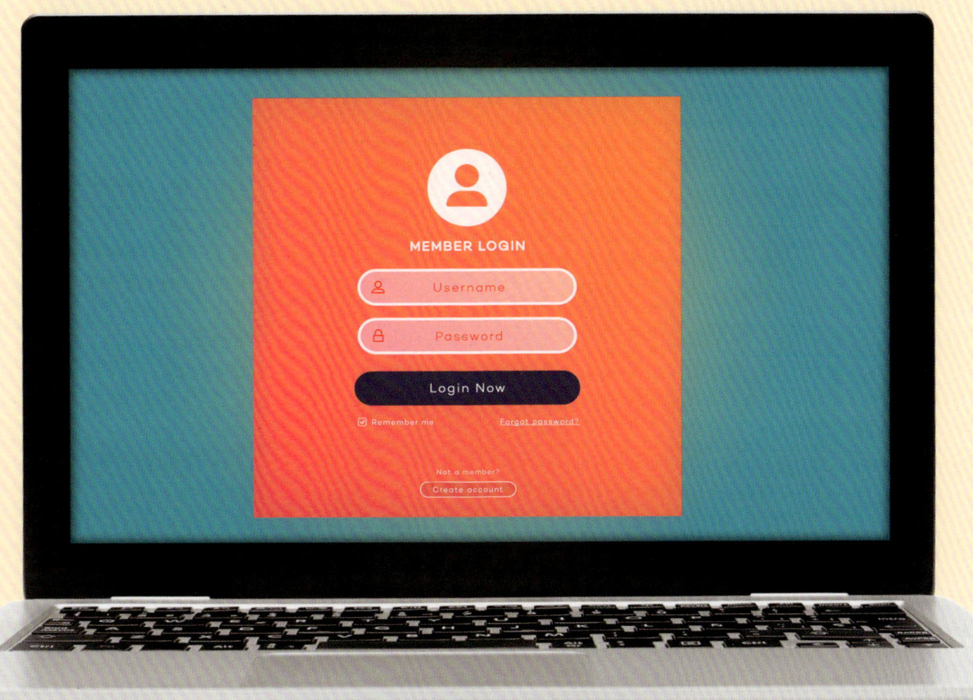

Have an adult make sure a site can be trusted before you make an account on it.

Many websites have rules to follow. Those rules are found on the website. They are on the site's **Terms of Use** and **Privacy Policy** page. Your parents and teachers can help you find these rules. Some popular sites have rules about age. They say users must be at least 13 years old. Those sites may want you to become a member. You might have to create an account. Even if you are old enough, ask a parent or guardian for permission before you create any accounts online.

If an advertisement makes you feel uncomfortable or unsafe, tell a trusted adult. That person will help you get out of it. You will learn how not to go there again.

Have you seen **advertisements** on websites? They are on the top or sides of pages. Sometimes they surprise you by popping up. They might be bright and colorful. They might say "You Won a Prize!" What happens if you click on them? You will end up at an advertiser's website. Do not be fooled. Do not click on these ads.

You can have lots of fun online. You can learn many things. Do you have friends or family who are far away? You can talk to them online. You can write stories. You can make movies. You can safely do all this and more. Just use the safety tips in this book. Have fun!

Try This

Passwords are important. They protect your account from other people. Can you create a password that follows these rules?

1. At least 8 letters and numbers long
2. A mix of letters and numbers
3. Does not include your name, age, pet's name, or anything else that someone could guess

Try making a sentence. Turn it into a password using the first letter from each word in the sentence. Replace some of the letters or words with numbers. For example, "The dog liked to leave the house before me," could be "TDL2LTHB4M." Make sure it is something you can remember!

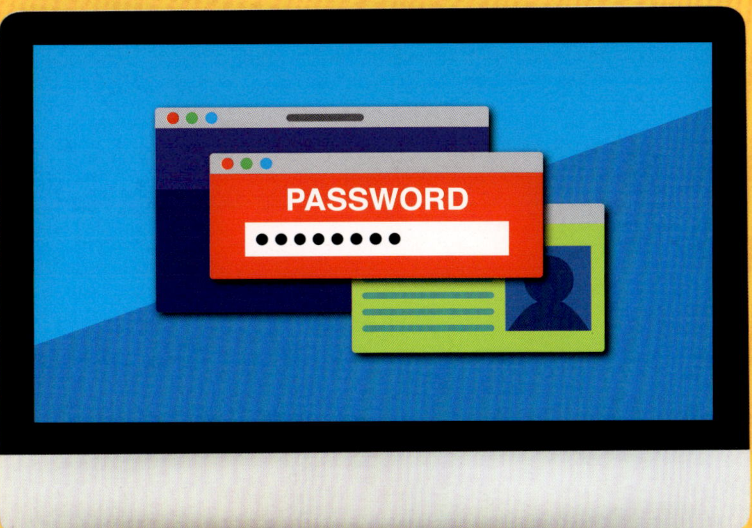

Always ask permission before creating an account.

Quiz

1 What is the name for the set of rules someone must follow to use many school computers?

2 What does privacy mean?

3 Who should you ask if you are unsure about anything you find online?

4 When was the personal computer developed?

5 Where is Drexel University?

6 What percent of U.S. classrooms regularly use desktop computers?

7 How many numbers and letters should be in a good password?

8 What do many libraries have that can help children find things online?

9 When did the internet become widely available?

10 Who can read words and see photos that you post to the internet?

Answers: 1. Acceptable Use Policy **2.** Keeping some things to yourself **3.** An adult **4.** In the 1970s **5.** Philadelphia, Pennsylvania **6.** More than 75 **7.** At least eight **8.** Databases **9.** In the early 1990s **10.** Anyone

Key Words

Acceptable Use Policy: rules that restrict how technology may be used

advertisements: paid announcements meant to sell something

bookmark: a website address stored on a computer so that the user can easily return to the site later

databases: sets of related information that are grouped together in one location in a computer

internet: the electronic network that allows millions of computers around the world to connect together

online: connected to other computers through the internet

privacy: keeping others from knowing your thoughts or words

Privacy Policy: a statement of how a website shares or collects information about visitors

reliable: trustworthy or dependable

search engines: computer programs that help you find words or information you request

Terms of Use: a collection of rules for using a website and reasons why your access to a site can be discontinued

Index

LIGHTBOX

SUPPLEMENTARY RESOURCES

Click on the plus icon found in the bottom left corner of each spread to open additional teacher resources.

- Download and print the book's quizzes and activities
- Access curriculum correlations
- Explore additional web applications that enhance the Lightbox experience

LIGHTBOX DIGITAL TITLES

Packed full of integrated media

VIDEOS

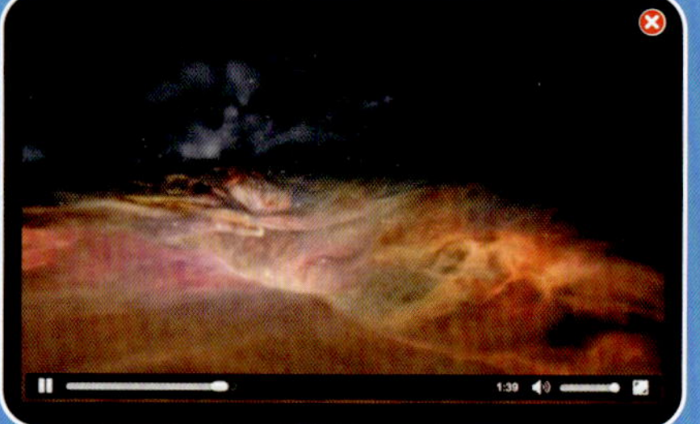

INTERACTIVE MAPS

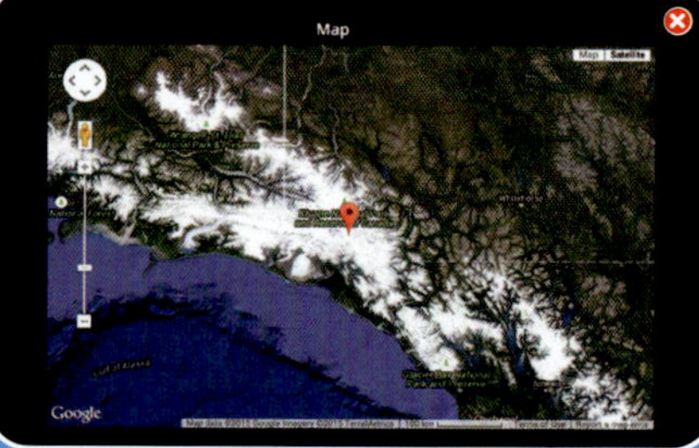

WEBLINKS

SLIDESHOWS

QUIZZES

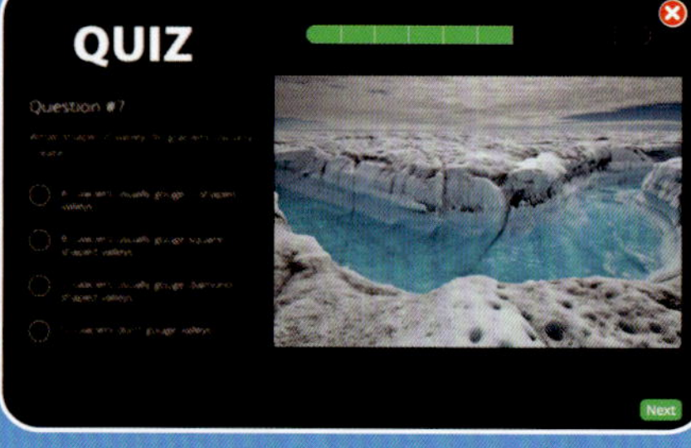

OPTIMIZED FOR

- ✓ TABLETS
- ✓ WHITEBOARDS
- ✓ COMPUTERS
- ✓ AND MUCH MORE!

Published by Lightbox Learning
276 5th Avenue
Suite 704 #917
New York, NY 10001
Website: www.openlightbox.com

First published by Cherry Lake Publishing in 2012

Library of Congress Control Number: 2021939468

ISBN 978-1-5105-5576-1 (hardcover)
ISBN 978-1-5105-5577-8 (multi-user eBook)

Printed in Guangzhou, China
1 2 3 4 5 6 7 8 9 0 25 24 23 22 21

082021
111020

Project Coordinator John Willis
Designer Jean Faye Marie Rodriguez

Photo Credits
Every reasonable effort has been made to trace ownership and to obtain permission to reprint copyright material. The publisher would be pleased to have any errors or omissions brought to its attention so that they may be corrected in subsequent printings.

The publisher acknowledges Getty Images and Shutterstock as its primary image suppliers for this title.